Sermons

on the

Mountain

F. E. GREENE JR.

ISBN 979-8-88685-596-8 (paperback)
ISBN 979-8-88685-598-2 (hardcover)
ISBN 979-8-88685-597-5 (digital)

Christian Faith Publishing
832 Park Avenue
Meadville, PA 16335
www.christianfaithpublishing.com

Printed in the United States of America

If thou shalt confess with thy mouth the Lord Jesus
and shalt believe in thine heart that God hath raised
him from the dead, thou shalt be saved.

Preface

Sermons on the Mountain was written and navigated by that continuing urge that kept resurfacing in the back of my mind. It's like a series of testimonies revealing my personal walk through life!

If the truth be told, I wasn't saved all my life! For I have many skeletons in my closet as you will read. And I believe *Sermons on the Mountain* will attract millions of curious readers.

Nonetheless, each aspect or episode of this book was written in the old-fashioned way, with pen and paper.

Navigated—solely! From that urgent desire of my crying out my life struggle. How sin got a hold of my life!

Come with me now as we witness some of these self-told sermonettes I call *Sermons on the Mountain.*

Foreword

My personal testimony began while I was still a young man. I navigated them firsthand through an open acknowledgment of my experiences by way of a series of sermonettes!

I wasn't fortunate enough to attend any four-year school of theology, and I don't have any dignitary titles such as *reverend* or *pastor* before my name. The following revelations were revealed to me in a monologue fashion—addressed to a sinner man!

And I heard a voice say, "Go ye therefore and teach all nations, baptizing them in the name of the Father and the Son and of the Holy Ghost. Teaching them to observe all things whatsoever I have commanded you. And lo, I am with you always, even unto the end of the world!"

And my Bible tells me that Jesus said, "Come ye after me, and I will make you fishers of men."

Chapter I

The small storefront church that recently moved into the neighborhood was my first experience with any kind of religion.

It was on a hot July Friday evening. When I inquisitively entered this church, inside, I saw a group of people gathered, singing and worshipping!

As I took a seat in the rear row, I noticed this old lady who stood about four feet tall. She was testifying, speaking about how fire shot up in her bones and how it was motivating her soul! Although she was a small figure of a woman, her voice sounded voluminously loud. She yelled, "When I first found Jesus!" Then I heard her say, "No, no! That's a lie because my Jesus was never lost!" She then rephrased her statement, "When my Jesus first found me, I was deeply buried in sin!"

She then raised both wrinkled arms high over her head. Tears were now running down her face. She continued, "I was so buried in sin! I was tired of living but afraid of dying!" She paused before saying, "My Jesus had to reach way down to pick me up! He sits by my feet on solid ground!" Crying out loud now, she began to pray, "I thank you, Jesus! I thank you, Lord."

This old lady was praying about her personal experience of life and suffering and sorrow! "Love and judgment, grace and hope! Justice and mercy! Through it all! That's what he has done for me!" she proclaimed.

Just then, a voice from the pulpit shouted out, "Go ahead, sister! Tell us what Jesus has done for you!"

I sat back in the rear row almost spellbound. I witnessed this old lady as she looked over near where the pianist and organist were stationed, and she yelled, "Come on, musicians! Help me sing this song! 'Cause I believe that singing is as close to worshipping as breathing is to life."

She then started singing, "When the storms of life are raging—in the midst of tribulation! When I'm growing old and feeble, Jesus, will you stand by me?"

Never before had I witnessed so few people caught up in the spirit. Their bodies were moving. Some were shouting and clapping their hands. Others were dancing to a Holy Ghost two-step while the pianist and organist played the song "Stand by Me." I was overwhelmed that day! That old lady's testimony and song got the best of me! At the conclusion of that song, I heard a voice from the pulpit saying, "Come if thou shalt confess with thy mouth the Lord Jesus! And if thou shalt believe in thine heart that God hath raised him from the dead, thou shalt be saved."

I gave my life to Christ that Friday evening. And straightaway, I left that old storefront church with the determination to go out into the world and spread God's Word! I was on fire for the Lord! "Hallelujah! Hallelujah to his name!"

When I arrived back within the privacy of my home, I secretly went into my closet and kneeled and began to pray, "Our Father, who art in heaven, hallowed be thy name! Thy kingdom come; thy will be done on earth as it is in heaven. Give us this day our daily bread, and forgive us our debts as we forgive our debtors. And lead us not into temptation but deliver us from evil, for thine is the kingdom and the power and the glory forever. Amen."

When I had prayed that prayer, I went out into the world for some forty years! I did everything and anything I was big enough to do!

I tried running away from Jesus. I was hiding on the backside of his word. I was in and out of several marriages. I am tainted with adultery! I was living my life so corruptibly!

I had no conscience about right and wrong. I was a wrath unleashed! At this point in my life, I rarely attended church. I was so consumed in sin that I thought I would live forever!

Then something happened. It was Easter Sunday morning when I visited this little missionary Baptist church.

Mostly, I was there to show off my Easter outfit! After all the children had made their speeches, the preacher got up to deliver the word. In his sermon, I felt like he was stepping all over my toes. He stated, "If it wasn't for the Lord on my side, tell me what would I do!" He then made eye contact with me before singing, "Father, I stretch my hand to thee. No other help I know." At that point, I was unable to maintain my composure. The preacher then shouted, "Sinner man! Sinner man!" He pointed at me then continued, "If I was you, I would give my life to Christ!" He then went through a long list of reasons why I should give my life to Christ before calling, "If you're overcome with burden, come! If your body needs healing, *come*! If you can't see your way out—have no way to go—*come*! If you've been treated very cruelly, often forsaken, and feel discouraged, *come*! If you need reassurance and are worried about your tomorrow, please *come*! If you want a good recipe for happiness!

That preacher set a fire under me that day. I recommitted my life to Christ. Six months later, I was ordained as a deacon and went on fire studying God's Word. The chorus came, and I began singing, "O Lord, I'm on my way. O Lord, I'm on my way. O Lord, I'm on my way home! If religion was a thing that money could buy, the rich would live, and the poor would die! Thank God Almighty! That ain't so because if the rich don't pray, to hell they'll go! O Lord, I'm on my journey. O Lord, I'm on my journey. O Lord, I'm on my way home!"

Six months later, I stood before this small church congregation and said, "Blessed are they which do hunger and thirst after righteousness, for they shall be filled."

I then continued, "Guide me, O thou great Jehovah! Pilgrim through this barren land, bear me through the swelling current but land me safe on Canaan's side. May we pray to the God of Abraham, Isaac, and Jacob—Lord of all that was, that is, and all that is to *come*! God who reached back and took nothing and made a world! God who planted the stars and hung both the moon and the sun! God who created time and dragged it through man's life and demanded time to be eternity! God bless all our going out and our coming in from this time forward! Amen.

"Church, would you open your Bibles with me to Numbers 13:1. And the Lord spake unto Moses concerning the journey to the promised land! My brothers and my sisters, if you would allow me, I would like to use the journey to the promised land as my topic."

I paused and then continued, "In this fifth book written by Moses, we find a travel diary telling of a journey made by a group of people that could have taken only eleven days! Yet it lasted for forty years! Church, I am talking about a journey to the promised land!

"My Bible tells me, shortly after this group of people departed from Egypt, shortly after crossing the Red Sea, shortly after having experienced the worst of tragedies, these people began to murmur. Their murmurings turned into complaints! Their complaints incited a rebellion! In other words, there was hell on this Christian's journey!

"Satan packed his bags, gave the old man trouble, and opened invitations to come along for a ride!

"Now one would think the Israelites would have more of a sustaining faith! After all, *they had just witnessed* the ten plagues God had placed on the Egyptians and Pharaoh.

"*They had just witnessed* how God had parted the Red Sea! *They had just witnessed* the pillar of cloud and the pillar of fire that God had placed before them as a guide.

"Still the Israelites continued complaining! Yet when they were hungry, God dropped manna bread to them from heaven! When they were thirsty, God made water come from a rock! When they needed some encouragement in times of storms, God was right there by their side.

"Church! Satan then began using every trick in the book to block the Israelites' path to the promised land. The Israelites had problems with drugs, so old Satan came and gave them a fix!

"Those Israelites who had problems with alcohol, old Satan gave them a drink! And all those complainers and mumblers were giving Moses more trouble than any man could bear! My Bible tells me, glory be to God! These Israelites were experiencing an outrageous rebellious revolution, an attack against God's guidance.

"In other words, the Israelites were failing to yield to God's guidance through Moses! In other words, they were refusing to continue to follow Moses's instructions of God's command! Church, we as a people today could take a lesson in how my God guides his people!

"I would like to pause right here and remind this congregation that I am talking about this journey to the promised land!"

I paused. "God's divine guidance to us is the Holy Bible, which is the rule book of our faith! As children of God, we should have some knowledge of God! We should know, glory be to God, what pleases him and what displeases him!

"Church, there is no substitute for walking with God and keeping his commandments! Because of their disobedience to God's word, there is no substitute for talking to God through the Holy Spirit on their journey to the promised land. Only Caleb and Joshua, among some six hundred thousand men, lived to enter Canaan.

"My Bible tells me that Miriam and Aaron both died because of their failure. Moses himself sinned by failing to give God credit for the miracle of water! It cost Moses his life!

"Church, there is great danger in disobeying God's word! In the words written in Isaiah 43:2, 'When thou passest through the waters, I will be with thee; and through the rivers, they shall not overflow thee; when thou walkest through the fire, thou shalt not be burned; neither shall the flame kindle upon thee.'

"Church, journey to the promised land."

Upon completion of my message, the journey to the promised land, I had a yearning to sing.

"I'm pressing on! I'm pressing on to the other side, to the other side. I'm pressing on to the other side, to the other side. With Christ on board, with Christ on board, you know I'm satisfied! You know I'm satisfied."

The church joined in singing with such compassion. I went straightaway from that little church, witnessing to a small group on a street corner. "They that trust in the Lord shall be like a mountain, which cannot be removed but abideth forever." I paused before continuing, "For our help is in the name of the Lord, who made both heaven and earth!"

I paused again then said, "Let us pray! Eternal Father, Eternal Father, I call you Father because you're our Father! I come this evening, O God, to lift up your darling son, *Jesus*! To exhibit in our hearts our love! To express with our mouths our admirations! To confess to all the world that you're the one and only true God! Besides you, there is none other!

"Glory be to God, that you shower down rain—storms of salvation—and forever let us love one another as you have loved us!

"All these things I pray, in Jesus's name. Amen. First, giving all honor to my Lord and Savior, Jesus the Christ, who is the source of my strength in everyday life! And to each of you, good evening!"

I paused before saying, "Folks, there's a word, and it's found in Hebrews 11:1–6."

I read the passage, and after reading all six verses, I shouted, "Some theologists have said that this book was written by Paul. Other critics have proclaimed that the real author is unknown! Still some critics have said that these biblical verses have no mirage!" I paused then said, "All of that does not matter! As long as these words were inspired by God!

"Chapter 11, verse 1 begins by defining faith! And I quote, 'Now faith is the substance of things hoped for, the evidence of things not seen!'

"If you'll allow me, I will attempt to speak on the subject! People, where is your faith in God? Where is your faith in God?

Well, if faith is the substance of things hope for, then it's through faith that we believe that this world was framed by the Word of God!

"Then it's through faith that we believe in the beginning was the Word, and the Word was with God! And the Word was God! And the word became flesh! Then it's through faith! Glory be to God! He woke us up this morning and started us on our way!

"Once again, I ask, people, where is your faith in God? *Faith* like the woman with the issue of blood! *Faith* like Daniel, who survived in the lions' den all night long, unharmed! *Faith* like those three Hebrew boys who survived in that fiery furnace, unharmed! *Faith*, glory be to God, like Moses, when his back was against the wall, he held out his staff and God parted the Red Sea!

"*Faith* like Sarah, though she was barren, she conceived a child in her old age! *Faith* like Noah, at the age of one hundred years old, built an ark!

"Through faith, we must believe and understand that God is the author and finisher of our faith! We must believe and conceive that this world was framed by the word of God! *Faith*, if not accompanied by action, is dead! *Faith*, if not deeply rooted in patience, will not survive!

"Faith in believing the scripture Romans 10:9, 'That if thou shalt confess with thy mouth the Lord Jesus, and shalt believe in thine heart that God hath raised him from the dead, thou shalt be saved!' Faith in believing that God so loved the world that he gave his only begotten son, that whosoever believeth in him should not perish but would have everlasting life! Once again, I ask, people, where is your faith in God?

"I become deeply moved each time I preach on faith and some of the people from the Bible! And I don't think I could continue preaching on faith without talking about Job!

"Here we find a man who had the best of both worlds! Job had all the riches money can buy! Job had a good family, many friends, but most of all, he had the love of God deep down in his heart!

"How many of you people standing here this evening know that every time you confess and repent and give your life to Christ, that's when the devil comes at us most? In other words, old Satan comes to tear down your faith!

"Satan may come at us in many ways! He may come disguised as that wife who sometimes gets on your last nerve! He may come disguised as that husband who sometimes says some of the meanest things! Satan may come as that child who just won't do right!

"Speaking of Satan, my Bible tells me that old Satan had the nerve to go before God to get permission to attack Job! Satan declared and said to God, 'Lord, I know you think you've got something in your servant Job! But if you let me have my way in his life, I will make him curse you to your face!'

"God answered Satan and said, 'Go ahead, Satan! Give it your best shot! But I demand you not take his life!'

"Old Satan went right to work. *Job's integrity* was challenged in the midst of suffering! In other words, we must stand up for something, or we will fall for anything!

"In Job's earthly world, all of his friends—even his wife—all turned against him! Yet in the midst of all his suffering, my Bible tells me that Job said, 'The Lord giveth, and the Lord taketh away! Blessed be the name of the Lord!'

"Job's faith, glory be to God, was put to the test! But I believe it was all part of God's master plan, knowing that—glory be to God!—just a little faith, as small as a grain of mustard seed, could move mountains! People, I'm talking about faith like that of Abraham, Isaac, and Jacob! Abraham, a man of faith who works. Isaac, a man of faith who endures. Jacob, a man of faith who wrestles!

"And my Bible tells me that it was Abraham who was promised by God that he would become the father of a great nation. It was Isaac who was used by God to test Abraham's faith! It was the patient faith of Jacob that refused to let go until he was blessed! People, where is your faith in God?

"As for me and my house, we're going to serve the Lord because I believe that my God can bring love out of hate! My God can pick up joy and guide it through my sorrow! My God can turn my night into day! He can talk to peace and demand that it range over all my troubles!

"My God—glory be to God!—can move all of my sickness and transform it into a cure! People of the streets, as I conclude my message, I would like to leave this in your spirit. Without faith, man the thinker loses his greatest thought! Without faith, man the worker loses his greatest motive!

"Without faith, man the sinner loses his greatest help! Without faith—glory be to God!—man the sufferer loses his fairest vision! And last but not least, man the mortal loses his only hope! My fellow brothers and sisters, before I leave you, I ask, where is your faith in God?"

Stepping forward into the crowd, I shouted, "Now unto him that's able to keep us all from falling to present us faultless! Before the presence of his glory with exceeding joy, to the only wise God, our Savior, be glory and majesty, dominion and power, both now and forever, let all God's people say amen!"

I left that street corner that day with my Bible in hand and still another sermonette on my mind. I couldn't waste any more time running away from God's command.

Two weeks later, at a Wednesday night Bible study class, I was asked to teach. I stood before the class and said, "The Lord is my light and my salvation. Whom shall I fear?" I asked. Then I said, "First, give all honor to Jesus the Christ who is the strength of my everyday life! To the angel of this house, my pastors, and to each of you, my brothers and sisters in Christ, good evening!

"This evening, our lesson could be found in your Bibles. In the book of Matthew—a gospel story of Jesus's life! Written by a Jew to these Jewish people!

"For those of you who have your Bibles, please open them with me to Matthew chapter 5, and I will begin reading verses 13 to 16."

After reading, I said, "This evening, our lesson title would be *Let your light so shine.* So let your light shine!

"My brothers and sisters, *Webster's Dictionary* defines the word *light* as something that makes vision possible! Like the sun, the moon, or maybe an electric light!

"This evening, for the sake of reasoning, I want to talk about a spiritual light that shines deep within thy soul! An illumination light that human eyes cannot see! An illumination light that Ezekiel refers to as 'fire that shot up in his bones'!

"An illumination light—glory be to God!—where Matthew wrote about as a comfort that would ease our griefs and give hope to all of our troubles! Folks, I am talking about a holy light that our Savior's blood could only reveal!

"Matthew the writer wrote here in this verse 13, 'Ye are the salt of the earth!' My brothers and sisters, salt is a flavor used to spice up our food! This scripture goes on to say, 'But if the salt'—talking about you and I—'have lost its savor, wherewith shall it be salted?'

"In other words, *if you and I* don't have the Word of God deep down in our hearts, *if you and I* have not accepted Jesus Christ as our

Lord and Savior, *if you and I*—glory be to God!—want to see Jesus, we must have that flavor from the Savior before our light can shine!

"I am reminded of a story about a young man who was out there in the world of sin! This young man lived his life like a burger king! He lived his life doing everything he was big enough to do!" I paused then continued, "I was this young man, and on every Friday and Saturday night, you could mostly find me at this one little nightclub doing my thing!

"What I found so unusual was that each time I would go to this nightclub, I would see this little old preacher moving among the crowd, talking to as many who would stop long enough for him to render a few words from the Bible! *Sometimes his words* would be from John 3:16, telling people how God so loved the world! *Sometimes his words* would be from Romans 10:9, saying what it takes to be saved!

"*Sometime his words*—glory be to God!—would be from John 14:6! The verse he caught me with says, 'Jesus is the way, the truth, and the life! If any man walks in the light, as he is in the light, the blood of Jesus Christ cleanseth us from all sin,' which is from 1 John 1:7.

"What the old preacher said to me that Friday evening had a profound effect on my life! I told you this story because I believe, with everything inside of me, that although that old preacher dwelled there in darkness, I believe he was letting his light shine!

"The problem most church folks face in letting their light shine is that most are unable to go out into these dark places and come out with their lights still shining bright! My brothers and sisters, I urge you this evening to let your light shine! In your homes, in your jobs, in your neighborhood—let your light shine!

"In that bad situation, when you were called everything but a child of God, in times of trouble, when your backs are against the wall, when in dying needs, when you've given up on life and feel so down and out, *let your light shine!*

"Church, I want to pause right here and give you five steps every true Christian must follow. And all five steps spell out J-E-S-U-S!

"The *first step* is the J—we must be born again if we want to see Jesus!

"The *second step* is the E—earnestly! We must ask God for forgiveness for our sins. My Bible says, 'Ask and it will be given!'

"The *third step* is the S—surrender thyself unto God! The apostle Paul wrote, 'Present your bodies as a living sacrifice!'

"The *fourth step* is the U—you must be willing to obey the spirit before you're allowed to let your light shine!

"And the *fifth step* is the S—surely you must believe that God died for your sins! And because of your belief, you're saved!

"Holy Spirit, my faithful guide! Manifest thyself in me that I may be more like Jesus! Holy Spirit, my faithful guide! Shine out in me my willingness to go out and shine in all nations, baptizing them in the name of the Father, the Son, and the Holy Spirit!

"Shine into the highways and byways of the world!

"Shine—glory be to God!—that my Lord will be glorified! Shine into the dark corners of sinner men's hearts! Shine that my Lord will be magnified!

"Tell the world that if you would confess with your mouth to the Lord Jesus—and believe in thy heart that God has raised him from the dead—you shall be saved, telling how my Lord was sacrificed!

"Shine, telling the world that Jesus is the way, the truth, and the life! No man cometh unto the father but by him! Shine, acknowledging God's promise when he said, 'In my Father's house are many mansions.' If it were not so, I wouldn't have told you!"

I paused before saying, "My brothers and sisters, as we bring this Bible study to a close, I would like to encourage each of you to let your light shine! Because I believe that God can change hate into love! He can change your dark night into day, all of your bitterness into sweetness!

"God can change your earthly pains into a Christian's gain! God can change you from being a victim of sin to an overcomer and victor in him!

"My God can change each of you from preying on folks to praying for folks! He can change all those who are poor in spirit for a reward in the kingdom of heaven!

"My God can change all those who are unworthy of grace and mercy! He can change all those repented hearts so that they may one day see God!

"As I close the book on our lesson, I would like to tell you a story about two old men—Grace and Mr. Mercy! One day, old man Grace called Mr. Mercy and asked, 'Mercy, how many souls down there are struggling with sin? And are there enough souls worthy that I might come down and dwell in their hearts? And what have you been doing to help these souls?'

"Mr. Mercy just shook his head and said, 'Grace, where were you? When my Lord came down to earth and died so that all may obtain mercy, was it not you that my Lord commissioned to follow in his footsteps to magnify thyself in grace? What have you been doing down there?'

"At that time, old man Grace had taken about all he could take from Mr. Mercy concerning his duties. Grace shouted, 'Wait a minute! God's grace is sufficient! His word is truth! And his reward is great! I was just calling to reinform you that we must continue to let our light shine!' Then he held up his hands and shouted, 'I ought to have some witnesses. Someone who is willing to stand up and shout out God's words!'

"At that time, Mr. Mercy said, 'What about *Abraham*? A man God chose to be the father of a great nation! What about Isaac? A promised child used by God! What about Jacob? A man who stole his brother's birthright. One who was so unworthy, yet God has a way of reaching down—picking out the worst—to do his will!' He paused, then continued, 'Come here, Peter! Because of your faith when you said, "You are the Christ! And upon this rock, I will build my church! And the gates of hell shall not prevail against it!" Come here, Job! A perfect and upright man. Although he lost everything, he remained faithful to the end! Class, let your light shine!'"

Two weeks later, I was at it again. I was preaching before a small group at a 9:00 a.m. prayer breakfast in the kitchen area, standing before a small podium. I said, "I was glad when they said unto me, let us go into the house of the Lord! Our feet shall stand within thy gate, O Jerusalem!

"Let us pray. We come before you this morning, O Lord, to ask your blessing upon this prayer breakfast! O Lord, anoint with your spirit all who would accept your preaching word that Jesus Christ be lifted up! And all may be drawn closer to him!

"Lord, fill us afresh with thy holy spirit! Unite us in fellowship of worship, and prepare us forever to love one another, for it's in Jesus's name we ask these things. Amen!

"If you have your Bible this morning, please open them with me to Genesis, chapter 12. I will read verses 1 to 3." When I finished reading the verses, I said, "I would like to use as a topic: when God makes a promise, hold on! When God makes a promise, hold on!

"*Webster's Dictionary* defines the word *promise* as a declaration—an expectation of something that is to come. In chapter 12 of Genesis, God calls Abram and said unto him, "Get up from your homeland and go unto a land. I will show you there. I will bless thee and make you the father of a great nation!

"Church, it's hard to be obedient to God's words when your life is outside of faith! It's hard to comprehend what God has promised when you're living in a world of sin! I just stopped by here this morning to tell you to be steadfast and obedient to God's promise! My Bible tells me how God went into detail telling Abram how he would father a child in his old age! Sarah, Abram's wife, overheard the talk of his promise! She laughs, saying, 'How can this be? I am way past childbearing age.'

"Sarah then conspired a plot to get her handmaiden to conceive this child that Abram's God had promised! In other words, Sarah didn't trust God at his word! But I came here this morning to tell you that *when my God makes a promise, you better hold on!*

"Anyway, after Sarah refused to accept God's word, the devil started to go up against God's promise! You'll know what happens when you give the devil a ride in your life! He would soon take over and drive! But you might ask, Mr. Preacher, how does the devil drive in your life? Well, I am glad you asked. He is driving when you yield to drinking alcohol! He is driving when you go to have that fix for drugs!

"He is driving when you have no love for your fellow man! He is driving—glory be to God!—when all your ways are dictated by sin! Church, don't let the devil drive! Stand on the Word of God!

"And my Bible tells me that with that promise, Abram never stopped to look back! Church, there is great danger in looking back! By looking back, you might be hindered and trip over something in front of you!

"By looking back, you might stir up your past that could come forward and mess up your future! Jesus himself said, 'No man having put his hand to the plough and looking back is fit for the kingdom of God.'

"Church, I need to stop right here and call your attention to this promise! It didn't happen all overnight! Although this promise was given to Abram, it was passed down to Isaac. It manifested itself with Abraham's grandson Jacob! But it didn't stop there. Abraham's great-great-grandson Joseph, some four hundred years later, while in Egypt on his deathbed, made his son Ephraim promise, saying, 'When my God leads his people into the promised land, please take up my bones and carry them with you! *Because when God makes a promise, hold on!*

"Hold on! When this life deals you a bad hand and everything goes wrong, *hold on*! When that illness you have where the doctors have said they can't do you any good, *hold on*! Glory be to God! When you're at that point in your life where you feel so all alone!

"When you're under deep life pressure, church, I encourage you to cast all care upon him who cares for you. And I strongly declare that you expand your understanding of God! Church, God will keep you in perfect peace if you keep your mind on him! Expand your gaze to God, focusing solely to Jesus, the author of our faith!

"Expand your ability to hear from God! In other words, the Lord speaks to those who listen. He speaks by way of the Holy Spirit! Expand your talk with God daily. We should forever pray and glorify his name!

"Church, I am glad this morning that I believe God for his promise! Will you trust him? Will you give him praise? Will you wait on his promise?

"One of the most important decisions anyone can make during their lifetime is to settle in their hearts to accept Jesus Christ as our Lord and Savior! If you don't remember anything about my preaching today, *please* remember: When God makes a promise, you better hold on! When God makes a promise, you best hold on! I thank you, and may heaven smile upon you."

Two weeks later, I found myself hosting our Wednesday night Bible class.

"Greetings once again. First, give all honor to my Lord and Savior, who truly is the strength of my everyday life!

"May we pray, enteral Father, enteral Father! I call you, Father, because you're our Father! We've come this evening to study your Word and give you praise! For you are worthy to be praised! I ask that you will touch thy people! That thy Words be accepted in our hearts and bring joy to our souls! Speak now as only you can! That thy Word will become flesh in our hearts and food for our souls! All these things we pray, in Jesus's name. Amen!

"Class, I am excited this evening to speak to you from Revelation 21:1–4." When I finished reading the verses, I said, "This evening our lesson title is *painting a picture of eternal life!*

"We find here in verse one, where John the writer wrote, 'And I saw a new heaven and a new earth!' Class, if I could give you a quick catch-up version of how John got here to the writing of this first verse!

"I can assure you that John wasn't writing on his own free will! John wrote while in a trance! If only I could use my holy ghost's imagination! John wrote as if he was placed in front of a large screen—like a television—that was powered by the Holy Spirit! What an experience that must have been!

"God himself dictated this vision to John through Christ by an angel. Class, chapter 21 was written after Christ had addressed the seven churches, the seven plagues, the seven angels blowing the trumpets, and the seven empty bowls of God's wrath of destruction!

"For the scripture said, 'For the first heaven and the first earth were passed away and there was no more sea!' No more crying and heartaches! No more confrontation with trials and tribulations! No more troubles—glory be to God!—would I have to induce!

"I want to stop right here and tell you that in this earthly world, which we live in, we're forever anticipating painting good pictures for our lives! Take, for example, our young school-age kids! Most of them could tell you the story of the three little pigs and how each little pig built their houses out of straw, sticks, and bricks!

"This three little pigs' story—in its childlike setting—reveals how that one pig that built his house out of bricks withstands and lasts! Class, if you build your trust in Jesus, your life too will last!

Likewise, in our modern day business world, many large companies, such as Enron, WorldCom, and others, are listed on the New York Stock Exchange and all exhibit financial pictures! Some aren't worth the papers their figures are written on!

"The insurance industry, a world superpower in itself, spends millions of dollars each year in training on how to go out and get the sale! They use a guide—what is called a mortality table! A measure used to predict and paint its company's financial picture!

"Class, I stopped by here this evening to also paint you a picture. Not like that of Enron or WorldCom or that of the three little pigs! Class, I've come to paint you a picture of eternal life! A picture—glory be to God!—of heaven, where heartaches and pains have no meaning! A picture where every day will be like Sunday! Each day is sweeter than the day before!

"Getting back to the scripture, verse 2 reads, 'And I, John, saw the holy city, new Jerusalem, coming down from God—out of heaven—prepared as a bride adorned for her husband!' *Painting a picture of eternal life!* Class, unlike most paintings, this picture I am referring to is not an abstract picture—one which might leave you scratching your head, trying to determine its meaning!

"This picture is not an everyday watercolor mirror—one which you might pick up from your local Walmart store.

"This picture—glory be to God!—is not a still life painting, something frozen in time! This picture, which John spoke of, is alive! It is filled with eternal life! I am talking about Jesus—Mary's baby, our bright and morning star!

"If I could use my holy ghost's imagination here, *first*, I would use a strong color called Come to Him Just as You Are!

"*Second,* I will brush on a combination of two colors called repentance and forgiveness!

"*Third,* I'll paint on the power of prayer and base it with grace and mercy!

"*Fourth,* knowing Christian folks as I do, I'll touch up this painting with a color I'll call Take One Day at a Time! Wait a minute here, class! Before I put the finishing touches on this picture, I want to caution everyone here—under the sound of my weak voice! Once you decide to accept this painting, I can assure you that your life won't be a bed of roses!

"There will be times on this Christian journey when worldly problems will stack the decks of life against you.

"There will be times when your day-to-day battle with sin is more than you can stand.

"There will be times—glory be to God! Even your faith will dip a little low, and you will feel so all alone!

"And I heard a great voice out of heaven saying, 'Behold the tabernacle of God is with you.'

"When the storms of life are raging!

"In the midst of our faults and our failures!

"Class, I believe when John wrote Revelation 22:1, 'And he showed me a pure river of water of life, clear as crystal, proceeding out of the throne of God. A well of water springs up into everlasting life!'

"Class, I believe this verse tells of the end-time! When grace and mercy shall be no more, the beginning of destruction will be divided into six seals. The first seal is the white horse. Its rider is conquering worldly kingdoms (Rev. 6:1–2).

"The second seal is the red horse that will bring civil wars and human unrest throughout the world (Rev. 6:3–4)!

"The third seal is the black horse. Its rider fills the earth with famine—food shortages!

"The fourth seal is written in Revelation 6:9–11," I read the verses, then continued speaking. "I, John, saw all of the souls—martyrs—those who gave their lives for Christ.

"Class, this book and the other books of the Bible reveal biblical stories, giving us a retrospective view of man's past life! Painting a picture of eternal life!" I paused and spoke again, "Painting a picture of eternal life! Class, dismissed."

One week later, I was back again for Wednesday night's Bible class. I opened the class by saying, "Jesus said, 'I am the way, the truth, and the life! No man cometh unto the Father but by me!' Let us pray! Our Father, our Father, we come this evening to lift up your darling son, Jesus! To exhibit in our hearts our love! To express in our minds our admiration. To confess with our mouths that you're the one and only true and living God! And besides you, there's none other!

"I ask—glory be to God!—that you shower down a rainstorm of salvation! And forever, let us love one another as you have loved us! All these things I ask in Jesus's name. Amen!

"Class, please open your Bibles with me to the book of Jeremiah, chapter 4, and I will begin reading verses 1 to 4." I paused after reading. "The lesson topic I will use is: *Have you tried the man called Jesus?* Have you tried the man called Jesus? In our text, Jeremiah the writer was forewarning the Jewish people how God would send the Babylonian armies to punish them because of their ungodly ways!

"Jeremiah went as far as to mention their punishments if they would not turn away from their idolatrous ways! In other words, they didn't line up with the Word of God! Many of us today are very much like those Jews of Jeremiah's time.

"They were willing only to accept God's Word in little bits and pieces! What do you mean by little bits and pieces, Mr. Teacher? Well, I am glad you asked. One example of bits and pieces is all the different denominations in the world today! Each denomination interpreted God's Word in bits and pieces—adopting only one set of scriptures over another!

"Class, you must accept the whole Word of God! Ninety-nine and a half won't do!

"You can't just love your brothers and sisters on Sunday morning! And hate their guts on Mondays, Tuesdays, Wednesdays, Thursdays, Fridays, and Saturdays!

"And you shouldn't allow yourselves to hold on to those sinful things that please you most! Jeremiah goes on and write (now this is God talking), 'If thou wilt return, o Israel, unto me and if thou wilt put away thine abominations out of my sight, then shalt thou not remove.' What God is saying here in the scripture—glory be to God!—if ye would repent, put away all your sinful ways and try my son, Jesus!

"Class, *Abraham* tried him and was made the father of a great nation! *Moses* tried him, God opened up the Red Sea! *Jacob* tried him—glory be to God!—while in a strange land. God changed his name, and he became the father of the twelve tribes!

"The three *Hebrew boys* tried him when they were put into a fiery furnace! *Daniel* tried him while in the lion's den. *Joseph* tried him, although his brothers sold him into slavery, God fixed his heart so that he forgave them!

"Class, I stopped by this evening to tell you that I had tried him! And I found the man to be alright!

"My question to you is: Have you tried this man called Jesus? Now the scripture said here in verse 2, 'That you can try him in *truth!* That you can try him in *judgment!* And you can try him in *righteousness;* And all the nations shall bless themselves in him, and in him shall they glory.'

"Class, when you repent of your wicked ways, be for real! Jeremiah prophesied to inspire all Christians to forever persevere the Gospel—word of Jesus—even in times when hardships and disasters may strike! We should forever be willing to go out and spread God's Word!

"*Matthew* went out to the Jews! *Mark* took the lone road and preached to the Romans. *Luke* carried his message to the Greeks. While *John* went out to the Gentiles. Class, there's a high price one must sometimes pay for spreading God's Word!

"My Bible tells me that Jeremiah became very unpopular for spreading God's Word! He was hated by kings, princes, and priests! Even the entire nation of Jews just for spreading God's Word!

"Class, you can't effectively tell someone how to get up out of sin unless you yourself were once down!

"You couldn't possibly know the goodness of Jesus until you first tried his love! Again, I ask, have you tried this man they call Jesus? Class, have you tried this man they call Jesus? Class dismissed."

Two weeks later, I received an invitation from the pastor of one of our sister churches to speak at their men's day anniversary. That Sunday, I stood before a crowded congregation and began singing: "I don't feel no ways tired! I've come too far from where I started from! Nobody told me that the road would be easy! I don't believe he brought me this far! I don't believe he brought me this far! Again, I don't believe he brought me this far to leave me!

"Church! I would like to talk about his journey to the promised land! Journey to the promised land! In our text, Moses leads a group of Jewish people on their way to the promised land.

"A journey that could have taken eleven days lasted, my Bible says, forty long years! On this forty-year journey, there was much disobedience and backbiting against God's word! In other words, there was hell on this journey!

"Church, this morning, I too was on a journey! And I am not ashamed to tell you that on my journey back when I was a young man, I went through hell traveling on my journey!

"In our texts, the Jewish people had traveled through numerous complaints against Moses—who was led by God's law! Their grumblings and murmurings soon turn to rebellion! Some even began serving other gods!

"Church, Isn't that the way we are today? We spend most of our time traveling through life, serving worldly things! Looking back over my life, after I gave my life to Christ, I backslided, went out into the world, and began doing everything sinful I was big enough to do!

"Still, my God was like Motel 6, he left the light on, so I could find my way back to him! In our text, God left the light on for those Jewish people! So they, too, could find their way back.

"By day, he supplies a pillar of cloud! And by night, he supplies a pillar of fire! On this journey to heaven, church, I stopped by here this morning to give you the direction to heaven!

"First, you must make a U-turn on that repentant road. In other words, repent of all your sins and give your life to Christ!

"Second, you must travel down the roads of Matthew, Mark, Luke, and John! Follow their footsteps and learn of their ways!

"Third, you must cross over that bridge over muddy water! Remember, once you give your life to Christ, the devil will attack you in many ways!

"Fourth, you must make a right turn onto that long, narrow highway! Some have called it the king's highway! Once on this king's highway, please take one day at a time!

"Wait a minute! According to my GPS biblical indicators, it said, up ahead you will approach a three-way intersection called Temptation Avenue, Fool's Road, and Hate Street. I caution you to guide your life like a vehicle through all three of these busy roadways! Onto the next, Jesus Boulevard all the way down in front of that building!

"Glory be to God! Not made by man! Once you reach this heavenly building, get up out of that earthly vessel, and go inside this building not made by man.

"Once inside this building not made by man, at the reception desk, you will find a man named King Jesus. At this point—glory be to God!—I want you to sit right down and tell King Jesus how you had to give up your rights to those who wronged you! How worldly pains had rocked your body that sometimes you had to cry all night! How—glory be to God—you were called everything but a child of God! Still you kept the cost! At this point, I want you to get on up and shout all over God's heaven!

"Shout for all of the struggles you had to endure! Shout for all of the heartaches and pains! Shout and say, 'I've made it! Thank God Almighty! I made it!'"

The following Wednesday evening, I opened our Bible study with these words: "I am the resurrection and the life, he that believeth in me! Though he was dead, yet shall he live! Greetings, class! This evening, I will speak about the resurrection of Lazarus!

"Let's pray. I was glad when they said unto me, 'Let us go into the house of the Lord!' For our feet shall stand within thy gates, o Jerusalem!

"Eternal Father, it's once again we come just to give you praise! For you're worthy of praise! We exalt you as King of kings and Lord of lords. We adore you as the lily of the valley, our bright morning star, and our sunshine on a cloudy day!

"Bless us now, o God, that we, too, will one day have a home in glory! Where every day will be like Sunday! Each day will be sweeter than the day before!

"Bless now, o God, as only you can bless now, as only you will! All these things we ask in the precious name of Jesus! Amen.

"For those of you who have your Bibles, please open them with me to the book of John, chapter 2. I will begin by reading verses 20 to 26: 'Then Martha, as soon as she heard that Jesus was coming, went and met him but Mary sat still in the house. Then said Martha unto Jesus, "Lord, if thou hadst been here, my brother had not died. But I know, that even now, whatsoever thou wilt ask of God, God will give it thee.'

"Jesus saith unto her, *'Thy brother shall rise again.'* Martha saith unto him, 'I know that he shall rise again in the resurrection at the last day.' Jesus said unto her, 'I am the resurrection and the life: he that believe in me, though he were dead, yet shall ye live. And whosoever liveth and believeth in me shall never die. Believest thou this?'

"I would like to use this as a title: *He is not dead!* Turn to your neighbor on your right and say, *'He is not dead.'* Now turn to your other neighbor on your left and say, 'He lives!'

"Class, we find here in this text an unfolding story of how death came and overtook a man named Lazarus! An emotional drama so intense that my Bible tells me—glory be to God!—that Jesus wept!

"Verse 20, B section says, 'As soon as Martha heard that Jesus was coming, she went out to meet him.' Then she said something so profound! She said, 'Lord, if thou hadst been here, my brother would not had died!'

"Turn to your neighbor again and say, *'He is not dead!'*

"Class, far too often, we have associated death with the absence of life! A state where time has no meaning! Where our minds and bodies cease to exist!

"Martha seems even more confused when Jesus says to her, 'Thy brother shall rise again.'

"*Martha* couldn't come to grips with the fact that her brother, who had been dead for four days, would be brought back to life!

"Martha couldn't comprehend that Jesus could bring Lazarus back to life on this side!

"Martha but then she didn't truly know who Jesus was! This Jesus was God! And is also 100 percent man! He was the same God that raised the widow's son from the dead (Luke 7:14)!

"This Jesus was the same God that spoke to the woman (Luke 8:52) and said, 'She is not dead but sleepeth!' And she came back to life!

"This Jesus—glory be to God!—was that same God that died on the cross for you and I! Went on down into the gates of hell! Defeated old death! Came back with all the power in his hand! Class, that's enough right there! I am about to have a holy ghost fit! Up in here! Getting back to verse 24, where Martha says, 'Lord, I know he shall rise again in the resurrection at the last day!'

"Now this is that part of the scripture where Jesus answers and says, 'I am the resurrection and the life! He that believeth in me, though he were dead, yet shall he live! And whosoever liveth and believeth in me shall never die!' Now Martha, I believe, was a praying woman! And she truly believed in her Lord and friend, Jesus!

"But bringing her brother back to life after four long days! Lord, by now, his body stinks! Martha wept. Jesus then asks, 'Where have ye laid him?' And my Bible said Jesus wept before calling out to Lazarus, 'Lazarus! Come forth!' And then Jesus said, 'Loose him and let him go!'

"And the crowd of Jews standing around all said, 'He's not dead!'

"Class, there is a lesson to be learned from this passage: we'll be, at one time, dead in sin—o, death, where is thy sting? O grave, where is thy victory?

"For the scripture said (1 Cor. 15:56) that the sting of death is sin! And the strength of sin is the law, but thanks be to God, who giveth us the victory through our Lord Jesus Christ!

"Class, in case you missed it, I am talking about the resurrection of Lazarus!"

One week later, I stood before that Wednesday Bible study class and began testifying: "First, I give all honors to my Lord and Savior, Jesus the Christ! To the angel of this house! And to each of you, my brothers and sisters in Christ, good evening.

"Class, there's something special in the name of Jesus! There's something mystical about calling the name *Jesus*! There is no other name—glory be to God!—that can bring sunshine into your life on a cloudy day!

"Calling Jesus can heal your sickness and can change your dark life into a bright one!

"Calling Jesus—glory be to God!—can forgive one of their sins and bring love from hate! It can pick you up when you're down and can talk to peace and demand it be still!

"*There's something special in the name of Jesus!*

"Calling Jesus, my Bible says, can transform your world of sins into a first-class ticket to be with him.

"Calling Jesus—glory be to God!—can bring food to your soul! It can create a new you!

"*There's something special in the name of Jesus!*

"His name is the sweetest name I know! Jesus, Jesus! Oh, how I love calling your name! When my troubles all surround me and I've got nowhere to go, Lord, you were right there to move my spirit!

"Jesus, Jesus, every day your name is the same! Acts 4:12, B-section said it is this way: 'For there is no other name under heaven given among men by which we must be saved.'

"Upon calling the name of Jesus, every knee in heaven, on earth and under the earth shall bow! And every tongue should confess that Jesus Christ is Lord.

"*There's something special in the name of Jesus!*

"According to *Webster's Dictionary*, a *name* is a designate assigned identity for a person, place, or thing! I stopped by this evening to tell you about a man named *Jesus*!

"He's Mary's baby! He's the King of kings, the Lord of lords! He's the son of the most high God!

"*There's something special in the name of Jesus!*

"There's salvation and joy in his name! There's happiness in his name! And every time I think of the goodness of Jesus—glory be to God!—I get all full inside! I can't contain myself! Class, I am about to have a holy ghost fit all up in here! It feels like a fire burning in my bones!

"Class, *there's something special in the name of Jesus!* Listen, David, the boy king, put it like this: 'The Lord is my shepherd; I shall not want.' Since giving my life to Christ, my God has redefined my needs and wants.

"'He maketh me to lie down in green pastures.' Class, while living within this world of _____!

"My God has enabled me to lie down in green pastures.

"Class, 'He leadeth me beside the still waters.' In troubled times, when the oceans of life are raging, my God guides me alongside the still waters.

"'He restoreth my soul.' Thanks, glory be to God! He renewed my soul! 'He leadeth me in the paths of righteousness for his name's sake.' In other words, my God leads me in accordance with his commandments for his name's sake!

"'Yea, though I walk through the valley of the shadow of death, I will fear no evil for thou art with me.' Class, with God on my side, I will never walk alone!

"'Thy rod and thy staff, they comfort me. Thou preparest a table before me in the presence of mine enemies! Thou anointest my head with oil-my cup runneth over! Surely goodness and mercy shall follow me all the days of my life: and I will dwell in the house of the Lord forever!'

"There's something special in the name of Jesus!"

And so it came to pass that the world was awoken to an Armageddon—series of viruses—a plague that affects more than 125 countries.

This pandemic's wrath preyed upon the people. And death spread it wings and multiplied itself into the millions! And the people cried out for help! And I heard a voice from heaven saying, "If my people, which are call by name, shall humble themselves, and pray, and seek my face, and turn from their wicked ways; then will I hear from heaven and will forgive their sin and will heal their land" (2 Chronicles 7:14).

"Class, if I could give a catch-up summary of what is happening in the midst of this pandemic crisis! The CDC (Centers for Disease Control and Prevention) conducted hours of clinical trials in search of a vaccine while people worldwide were dying by the millions!

"In other words, my brothers and my sisters, the people had turned away and forsaken God's commandments! They had put God to the sidelines of their lives! Many have gone to serve other gods!

"If God's people would discontinue their racial divide and start loving their neighbors as themselves!

"If his people—glory be to God!—would turn from their wicked ways!

"If his people would pray and ask for forgiveness and seek God's face then he will stop these pestilence, virus, and not close heaven!

"Class, if his people…"

Coming back after giving my life to Christ, I finally came to realize that I must continue to preach God's Word.

One week later, I stood before a Wednesday Bible study class and testified: "First, I give honor to my Lord and Savior, Jesus the Christ! To the angel of this house! And to each of you, my brothers and sisters in Christ, good evening.

"I am reminded of the story where this backwoods little country town had this old doctor who still made house calls!

"And everywhere this old doctor would go, you would see his old hound dog named Blue, following him. On this particular day, this old doctor was summoned to this elderly man's house who lived on the edge of town.

"Shortly, after the doctor entered the man's house, the old man quickly greeted him and replied, 'Doctor, doctor, I know I don't have long to live! I am afraid of dying! What can you do for me?'

"Just then, there was a scratching sound coming from the outside of the door. The doctor whispered, 'Listen, do you hear that? That's my dog, Blue! I am his master! And he's scratching because he wants to come in here and…'

"He paused before saying, 'Your ailment, sir, is scratching away at your life! You, sir, should feel fortunate enough to want to go on up to be with your master. Wait for the Lord! Wait, I say, for the Lord!'

"After that old doctor left that man that day, he went to visit this old man who lives in a little ramshackle house. In a wooded terrain, when he arrived, he found this elderly gentleman sitting on his front porch, rocking away in an old beat-up chair!

"The doctor spoke first and said, 'Ben, you've been around this neighborhood for a long time! Some of your neighbors have been complaining, wanting to know why are you hanging around living so long?'

"This old gentleman never stopped rocking! He held up an old, beat-up Bible. Its covers were peeling! He mumbled, 'Doc, I wait for my Lord! My soul does wait! And in his Word, I do hope.'

"Then this old man said something so profound! 'Doc, I read somewhere in this old Bible that Jesus was coming!'

"Tears were running down his face! He whispered, 'I know he's coming back because he came and took my wife one day! And this here the Bible says, "He will come again!"'

"The doctor then said, 'Ben, when God makes a promise, you best hold on!'"

Class after hearing those stories, I became so motivated just thinking what the Lord had done in my life! When I think of the goodness of Jesus and all that he had done for me, my soul, my soul—the inner voice of me—cried, 'Hallelujah, hallelujah! Thanks God for saving me! I thank you, Jesus! I thank you, Lord!

Father, I've come to that part of my life to give you all the praise! For you are worthy to be praised! I come knowing—glory be to God!—it could have gone the other way in my life—glory be to God!—But, thanks to your grace and mercy, you found favor in me!

I come trusting that God raised Jesus from the dead! I come confessing and believing in my heart! I come—glory be to God!—knowing that man believes in righteousness with his heart and confesses salvation with the mouth!

I come, Jesus, steadfast in faith in your Word! I come, I come with a continuous zeal to preach your Word!

This is your servant's prayer. Amen!

Class, I hope my teaching hasn't been in vain! These are my personal testimonials!

The end.

About the Author

F. E. Greene Jr. was brought up in and around the religious environment of the church. He was ordained a deacon at fifty, where he went on fire studying God's Word.

After two years, he received a revelation: to write *Sermons on the Mountain*, a testimonial series revealing his personal experiences in life.

When we first interviewed Deacon Greene, we asked him, "What prompted you to write this book, and what should we tell your readers? Who are you as a person?"

Deacon Greene said, "I wrote this book because of Jesus's great commandments, and if you must tell them anything, just tell them, I am a child of God!"

Deacon Greene has since continued writing other books:

- *A Walk Through the Bible*
- *Two Worlds Between Us*
- *Up Against a Giant*
- *Wheeler Hill—The Saga*
- *Colored People*
- *Sermons on the Mountain*

To purchase a copy of these books, go to Barnes & Noble bookstore or Amazon Books.